The Jackdaw of Rheims, by Thomas Ingoldsby

Richard Harris Barham

THE

JACKDAW OF RHEIMS.

He long lived the pride   Of that country side,
And at last in the odour of sanctity died.   P. 29.

THE

JACKDAW OF RHEIMS.

BY

THOMAS INGOLDSBY.

WITH TWELVE ILLUSTRATIONS, PRINTED IN COLOURS.

London:

RICHARD BENTLEY.

8, NEW BURLINGTON STREET.

1870.

LIST OF ILLUSTRATIONS.

And being thus coupled with full restitution,
The Jackdaw got plenary absolution! P. 23.

"Tunc miser Corvus adeo conscientiæ stimulis compunctus fuit, et execratio cum tantopere excarneficavit, ut exinde tabescere inciperet, maciem contraheret, omnem cibum aversaretur, nec ampliùs crocitaret : pennæ præterea ei defluebant, et alis pendulis omnes facetias intermisit, et tam macer apparuit ut omnes ejus miserescent." * * * * *

"Tunc abbas sacerdotibus mandavit ut rursus furem absolverent ; quo facto, Corvus, omnibus mirantibus, propediem convaluit, et istinam sanitatem recuperavit."

De Illvst. Ord. Cisterc.

JACKDAW OF RHEIMS.

———◆———

THE Jackdaw sat on the Cardinal's chair!

Bishop and abbot, and prior were there;

Many a monk, and many a friar,

Many a knight, and many a squire,

With a great many more of lesser degree,—

That little Jackdaw kept hopping about;
Here and there like a dog in a fair.

In sooth, a goodly company;

And they served the Lord Primate on bended knee.

Never, I ween,

Was a prouder seen,

Read of in books, or dreamt of in dreams,

Than the Cardinal Lord Archbishop of Rheims!

In and out

Through the motley rout,

That little Jackdaw kept hopping about;

Here and there

Like **a** dog in a fair,

Over **c**omfits and cates,

And dishes and plates,

Cowl and cope, **a**nd rochet and pall,

Mitre and crosier! he hopp'd upon all!

With saucy air,

He perch'd on the chair,

Where, in state, the great Lord Cardinal sat

In the great Lord Cardinal's great red hat;

The Jackdaw sat on the Cardinal's chair.

And he peer'd in the face

Of his Lordship's Grace,

With a satisfied look, as if he would say,

"We Two are the greatest folks here to-day!"

And the priests, with awe,

As such freaks they saw,

Said, "The Devil must be in that little Jackdaw!!"

The feast was over, the board was clear'd,

The flawns and the custards had all disappear'd,

And six little Singing-boys,—dear little souls

In nice clean faces, and nice white stoles,

Came in order due, Two by two

Marching that grand refectory through !

A nice little boy held a golden ewer,

Emboss'd and fill'd with water, as pure

As any that flows between Rheims and Namur.

Which a nice little boy stood ready to catch

In a fine golden hand-basin made to match.

The friars are kneeling, and hunting and feeling
The carpet, the floor, and the walls, and the ceiling.

Two nice little boys, rather more grown,

Carried lavender-water, and eau-de-Cologne;

And a nice little boy had a nice cake of soap,

Worthy of washing the hands of the Pope.

One little boy more

A napkin bore,

Of the best white diaper, fringed with pink,

And a Cardinal's Hat mark'd in "permament ink."

The great Lord Cardinal turns at the sight

Of these nice little boys all dress'd in white :

From his finger he draws

His costly turquoise ;

And, not thinking at all about little Jackdaws,

Deposits it straight

By the side of his plate,

While the nice little boys on his Eminence wait ;

Till, when nobody's dreaming of any such thing,

That little Jackdaw hops off with the ring!

*   *   *   *   *

A nice little boy held a golden ewer,
Embossed and filled with water, and pure.

There's a cry and a shout,

And a deuce of a rout,

And nobody seems to know what they're about,

But the monks have their pockets all turned inside out;

The friars are kneeling,

And hunting and feeling

The carpet, the floor, and the walls, and the ceiling.

The Cardinal drew

Off each plum-colour'd shoe,

And left his red stockings exposed to the view;

He peeps, and he feels

In the toes and the heels ;

They turn up the dishes,—they turn up the plates,—

They take up the poker and poke out the grates,—

They turn up the rugs,

They examine the mugs :—

But, no!—no such thing ;—

They can't find THE RING !

And the Abbot declared that, "when nobody twigg'd it,

Some rascal or other had popp'd in, and prigg'd it!"

When the Sacristan saw,   On crumpled claw,
Come limping a poor little lame Jackdaw!

The Cardinal rose with a dignified look,

He call'd for his candle, his bell, and his book!

In holy anger, and pious grief,

He solemnly cursed that rascally thief!

He cursed him at board, he cursed him in bed;

From the sole of his foot to the crown of his head;

He cursed him in sleeping, that every night

He should dream of the devil, and wake in a fright;

He cursed him in eating, he cursed him in drinking;

He cursed him in coughing, in sneezing, in winking;

He cursed him in sitting, in standing, in lying;

He cursed him in walking, in riding, in flying;

He cursed him in living, he cursed him in dying!—

Never was heard such a terrible curse !!

But what gave rise

To no little surprise,

Nobody seem'd one penny the worse !

The day was gone,

The night came on,

In holy anger, and pious grief,
He solemnly cursed that rascally thief!

The Monks and the Friars they search'd till dawn;

  When the Sacristan saw,

  On crumpled claw,

Come .imping a poor little lame Jackdaw!

  No longer gay,

  As on yesterday;

His feathers all seem'd to be turned the wrong way;—

His pinions droop'd—he could hardly stand,—

His head was as bald as the palm of your hand;

  His eye so dim,

So wasted each limb,

That, heedless of grammar, they all cried, " THAT'S HIM !—

That's the scamp that has done this scandalous thing !

That's the thief that has got my Lord Cardinal's Ring !"

The poor little Jackdaw,

When the monks he saw,

Feebly gave vent to the ghost of a caw ;

And turn'd his bald head, as much as to say,

" Pray, be so good as to walk this way !"

He hopp'd now about   With a gait devout;
At Matins, at Vespers, he never was out.

Slower and slower

He limp'd on before,

Till they came to the back of the belfry-door,

Where the first thing they saw,

Midst the sticks and the straw,

Was the RING, in the nest of that little Jackdaw!

Then the great Lord Cardinal call'd for his book,

And off that terrible curse he took ;

The mute expression

Served in lieu of confession,

And, being thus coupled with full restitution,

The Jackdaw got plenary absolution !

—When those words were heard,

The poor little bird

Was so changed in a moment, 'twas really absurd,

He grew sleek, and fat ;

In addition to that,

A fresh crop of feathers came thick as a mat !

Where the first thing they saw,   Midst the sticks and the straw,
Was the RING *in the nest of that little Jackdaw!*

His tail waggled more

Even than before ;

But no longer it wagg'd with an impudent air,

No longer he perch'd on the Cardinal's chair.

He hopp'd now about

With a gait devout ;

At Matins, at Vespers, he never was out ;

And, so far from any more pilfering deeds,

He always seem'd telling the Confessor's beads.

If any one lied,—or if any one swore,—

Or slumber'd in pray'r-time and happened to snore,

That good Jackdaw

Would give a great " Caw !"

As much as to say, " Don't do so any more !"

While many remark'd, as his manners they saw,

That they " never had known such a pious Jackdaw !"

He long lived the pride

Of that country side,

And at last in the odour of sanctity died;

When, as words were too faint

It's the custom, at Rome, new names to bestow,
So they canonised him by the name of Jem Crow!

His merits to paint,

The Conclave determined to make him a saint ;

And on newly-made Saints and Popes, as you know,

It's the custom, at Rome, new names to bestow,

So they canonised him by the name of Jem Crow !

LONDON:
R. CLAY, SONS, AND TAYLOR, PRINTERS,
BREAD STREET HILL.

LONDON:
R. CLAY, SONS, AND TAYLOR, PRINTERS,
BREAD STREET HILL.

Lightning Source UK Ltd.
Milton Keynes UK
UKHW030040241220
375792UK00007B/1294